Wild Weather

REVISED AND UPDATED

Catherine Chambers

Heinemann Library
Chicago, Illinois

© 2002, 2007 Heinemann Library
a division of Reed Elsevier Inc.
Chicago, Illinois

Customer Service 888-454-2279

Visit our website at www.heinemannraintree.com

Designed by Steve Mead and Q2A Creative
Maps by Paul Bale
Printed in China by South China Printing Company

11 10 09 08 07
10 9 8 7 6 5 4 3 2 1

New edition ISBN: 978-1-403-49577-8 (hardcover)
                     978-1-403-49586-0 (paperback)

The Library of Congress has cataloged the first edition as follows:
Chambers, Catherine, 1954-
 Flood / Catherine Chambers.
         p. cm. -- (Wild weather)
Summary: Introduces what floods are, conditions that exist during floods, their harmful and beneficial effects, and their impact on humans, plants, and animals.
Includes bibliographical references and index.
 ISBN 1-58810-651-9 (HC), 1-4034-0114-4 (Pbk)
 1. Floods--Juvenile literature. [1. Floods] I. Title. II. Series.
 GB1399 .C4797 2002
 551.48'9--dc21
                        2002000819

Acknowledgments

The author and publishers are grateful to the following for permission to reproduce copyright material: Aerial Archives/Alamy p14, AP Photo/Vincent Laforet, POOL p15, Ardea p5, Corbis pp16, 17, 23, 24, James Davis, Eye Ubiquitous/Corbis p29, Ecoscene pp4, 8, 10, 12, 25, EPA (PA photos) p22, Getty Images/PhotoDisc p28, Oxford Scientific Films pp9, 11, 19, PA Photos pp21, 27, Reuters p18, Reuters/Miro Kuzmanovic MIK p13, Rex Features p26, Robert Harding Picture Library p20, Still Pictures p7.

Cover photograph of floods in New Orleans, Louisiana, reproduced with permission of Radhika Chalasani/Getty Images.

The publishers would like to thank Mark Rogers and the Met Office for their assistance with the preparation of this book.

Every effort has been made to contact copyright holders of any material reproduced in this book. Any omissions will be rectified in subsequent printings if notice is given to the publisher.

The paper used to print this book comes from sustainable sources.

Some words are shown in bold, **like this**. You can find out what they mean by looking in the glossary.

Contents

What Is a Flood?

A flood happens when water covers land that is usually dry. Heavy rain makes river waters spill over their **banks**. Storms can make huge sea waves that flood the **coast**.

■ *These houses are on **stilts**. They are safe from the flood waters.*

■ *The water flooded streets and buildings.*

This city is in North Dakota. In April 2006, the waters of the great Red River burst its banks. People were forced to leave their homes.

Where Do Floods Happen?

Floods happen mostly where there are lots of storms. Storms bring heavy rain and strong winds. This can cause rivers to flood.

■ *The areas in blue are places where floods often happen.*

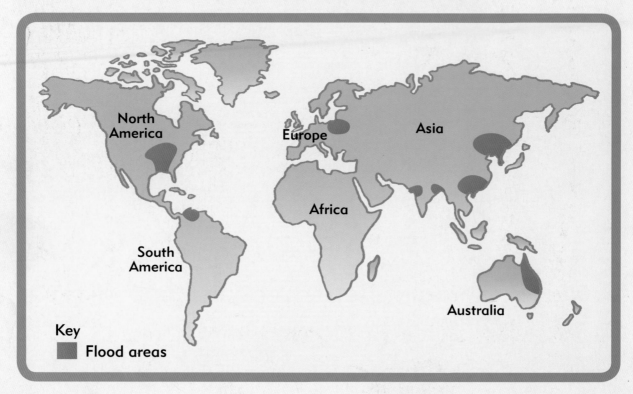

North America

Europe

Asia

Africa

South America

Australia

Key

Flood areas

■ *Floods often happen in Bangladesh.*

This flood is in the Asian country of Bangladesh. Bangladesh gets a lot of heavy rain from June to September each year. This time is called the monsoon season.

Where Does Rain Come From?

When winds blow over the oceans, they pick up tiny drops of **water vapor**. As air rises into the sky it cools and the water vapor turns into small droplets of water. These droplets make clouds.

■ *Clouds form above the oceans.*

■ *Rain falls from large dark clouds.*

If the droplets join together, they become too heavy and fall to the ground as rain. If there is too much rain in one place, it can cause floods.

Why Do Floods Happen?

This is a river **floodplain**. When heavy rain falls the river can become too full. The water rises above the **banks** and spills on to the floodplain.

■ *These fields are sometimes flooded by the river.*

■ *This coast is in danger of being flooded.*

Strong winds blow across the oceans during
storms. This makes the water into huge waves.
These rise over the shore and cause floods
along the **coast**.

What Are Floods Like?

Sometimes floodwaters rise slowly. People have time to get ready for the flood. At other times floodwaters rise quickly. People and cars get caught in the flood.

■ *This river is full and ready to burst its banks.*

■ *The inside of this house has been badly damaged by floodwaters.*

The water makes buildings and anything inside wet. Some things are washed away. The water also brings in a lot of dirt. This dirt has been picked up by the floodwaters.

New Orleans Flood

This is the city of New Orleans. It lies on low land near the **coast**. **Flood defenses** have been built to try and stop the city from flooding.

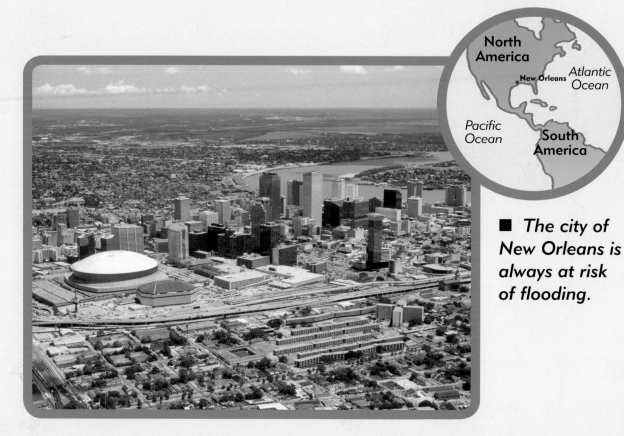

North America

New Orleans

Atlantic Ocean

Pacific Ocean

South America

■ *The city of New Orleans is always at risk of flooding.*

■ *Buildings in New Orleans were badly flooded in 2005*.

In 2005 a large storm, called a hurricane, made some huge waves. These waves broke the flood defenses and the city was flooded. People had to leave their homes.

Harmful Floods

Floodwaters can trap people and animals. Roads and bridges are flooded and broken. During a flood it can be harder to find fresh food or clean drinking water.

■ *Animals can be trapped by floodwaters.*

Huge waves have flooded this **coast**. Boats and buildings are damaged. Roads are covered in sand and stones. Fish, seabirds, and seaweed are washed up onto the shore.

Helpful Floods

In Bangladesh plants rot in the floodwaters. The rotted plants in the water help to make **fertile** soil. Rice **crops** grow well in this soil.

■ *Floods can be good to soil and crops in Bangladesh.*

A river flows very fast when there is a lot of rain. The fast river washes down a lot of mud. The mud settles on the flooded fields. This can make the soil in these fields more fertile.

■ *This river is picking up mud as it flows.*

Preparing for Floods

Weather stations ask radio and television stations to tell people about floods. The most serious warning is the **flood warning**.

■ *A flood warning tells people to get ready for floods.*

■ *These men are stacking sandbags along a riverbank in case it floods.*

People move their furniture upstairs. They switch off the electricity. Sandbags are stacked against doors and along rivers. This stops water from reaching houses. Some people leave their homes.

Coping with Floods

In some countries there are bad floods nearly every year. So **flood shelters** are built on high ground. People hurry to these shelters when there is a flood.

■ *Sometimes it is safer to stay in a shelter during a flood.*

■ *People have to travel by boat if roads are flooded.*

Floodwaters can cover roads for many days.
The water stops car and bus engines from
working. So people can only travel around
by boat or by air.

Living with Floods

This is an area that often floods. So people have built **platforms** on **stilts**. Cows, chickens, and other farm animals are kept safe until the floodwaters go down.

■ *These animals are safe from the flood.*

■ *Too much water can be bad for rice crops.*

Rice is a **crop** that grows in flooded fields, but heavy flooding destroys rice and other crops. They are battered by the flowing water. Then they rot in the ground.

To the Rescue!

The country of Mozambique was badly flooded in 2000. Helicopters rescued people from trees and high ground. They dropped food and equipment to make clean drinking water.

■ *People were rescued from trees by helicopters.*

■ *Boats can be used to rescue people from floodwaters.*

Lifeboats are used to rescue people from their flooded homes. The rescuers take the people to places that are above the flood. There they will find food and warmth.

More Floods?

Earth's climate is changing all the time. At the moment it seems to be getting warmer. This is called "global warming." Some scientists think that this will bring more floods.

■ *The white patches over Earth are clouds.*

■ *Warm weather causes snow and ice to melt.*

Scientists believe global warming will cause some of the ice in arctic regions to melt. This will raise the sea level and cause more floods in **coastal** areas.

Fact File

◆ The Huang Ho River in the country of China floods a lot. Flooding on the Huang Ho River has killed more people than any other floods. In 1931 nearly four million people drowned.

◆ In 2004 an earthquake in the Indian Ocean caused a huge wave called a tsunami. The wave flooded **coastal** areas in many countries. Over 200,000 people were killed.

Glossary

bank higher ground on either side of a river

climate usual weather in a part of the world

coast strip of land next to a large body of water

crop plant grown for eating, such as rice or wheat

debris remains of destroyed things

fertile good for growing crops in

flood warning warning when floodwaters become dangerous

flood defense barrier built to keep floodwaters from flowing onto the land

floodplain flat land along which a river winds

flood shelter building put up on high ground where people can escape floods

lifeboat boat built specially for rescuing people from dangerous waters

platform flat floor raised above the ground

stilts tall poles that hold up platforms or buildings

water vapor water that has changed into a gas

weather station where scientists work out changes in the weather

More Books to Read

Hughes, Monica. *Nature's Patterns: The Water Cycle*. Chicago: Heinemann Library, 2005

Royston, Angela. *The Weather: Rain*. Mankato, Minn.: Chrysalis Children's Books, 2004

Index